"Empire of Innovation: Unleashing the Entrepreneurial Spirit"

Willard T. Lewis

TABLE OF CONTENTS

INTRODUCTION

You are welcome to the exciting world of Entrepreneurship!

Entrepreneurship, What is this all about? One may ask.

Well, Entrepreneurship is basically about getting profits by putting to work your unique initiative and love for whatever you are passionate about . To be an entrepreneur, indeed, you need to be a good originator and developer of mind-blowing abilities and resources to enable you to work effectively in a high-productivity environment and circumstances.

Putting into consideration the present state of economic development and the percentage of employment rates across the country, one will concur that there is no better time to get engaged in the world of Entrepreneurship by putting to work whatever assets are caged up inside of us. Thus, when placing value on entrepreneurship, try to compare the benefits and obstacles of working for someone else and creating and running your own business.

When you weigh up the answers you got from the two comparisons, you will agree that creating and running your own business is more favourable than the latter. Now you will agree that each step taken in the world of entrepreneurship is worth it.

In this book, we will be:

- ★ Unveiling many unique, enticing, and ground-breaking ideas about entrepreneurship.
- ★ Learning about the things to do and not do will help us build and sustain an entrepreneurial empire.

★ Getting new methods of growing our entrepreneurial empire.

★ Learning how to overcome challenges in entrepreneurship and achieve success.

★ Knowing the impact of an entrepreneur in society and the world of business.

All these and many more are hidden in the pages of this book, so do not miss out on this opportunity to unleash the spirit of entrepreneurship in you to create a beneficial area for you.

I look forward to seeing you at the concluding part of this interesting ride into "Empire of Innovation: Unleashing the Entrepreneurial Spirit".

CHAPTER ONE

UNDERSTANDING "ENTREPRENEURSHIP"

Who is an Entrepreneur?

An entrepreneur is somebody who has a thought and who attempts to make an item or administration that individuals will purchase, as well as an association to help that work. A businessperson takes on the vast majority of the risk and drive for their new business and is, in many cases, considered a visionary or trailblazer.

Entrepreneurs are, however, different, as they may be dynamic.

There are a wide range of sorts of business visionaries, including entrepreneurs, content makers, startup pioneers, and any individual who has the desire to construct a business and work independently.

An entrepreneur is also called a business visionary because he or she is somebody who is energetic and inventive and makes another business. Their business doesn't have to waste time—your most loved neighborhood bistro is a business as well—but it takes an innovative outlook to rejuvenate their thoughts.

What are the various types of Entrepreneurs?

Only one out of every odd business person has something very similar, and not all have similar objectives. The following are a couple of types of entrepreneurs:

★ Developers:

Developers try to make versatile organizations within a short period of time.

Manufacturers normally pass $5 million in income in the initial two to four years and keep on developing until $100 million or past. These people try to work out serious areas of strength by recruiting the best talent and looking for the best financial backers. Some of the time, they have sensitive characters that are fit for the quick development they want yet may make individual and business connections troublesome.

★ Optimistic:

Sharp business people are hopeful people with the capacity to select monetary open doors, get in brilliantly, and remain on board during the hour of development, and leave when a business hits its pinnacle.

These entrepreneurs are worried about benefits and abundance they will construct, so they are drawn to thought of where they can make leftovers or recharging pay. Since they are hoping to find very well-planned open doors, pioneering business visionaries can be rash.

★ Innovator:

Innovators are those uncommon people who surface with an extraordinary thought or item that nobody has considered previously. Consider Thomas Edison, Steve Occupations, and Imprint Zuckerberg. These people chipped away at what they adored and tracked down business openings through their vision and thoughts.

Instead of zeroing in on cash, pioneers will generally think more about the effect that their items and administrations have on society. These people are not as awesome at maintaining a business as they are at creating people, so they frequently pass on the everyday tasks to those more able in that regard.

★ **Specialist:**

These people are scientific and take risks. They have serious areas of strength for a set in a particular region gained through schooling or apprenticeship.

An expert entrepreneur will work out their business through systems administration and references, here and there bringing about slower development than a developer business visionary.

Common traits for entrepreneurs include:

Entrepreneurs who are willing to build an empire in the world of entrepreneurship have traits that distinguish them from others. Some of these traits are:

★ Enjoy freedom and flexibility

★ Are inventive

★ Are goal-oriented and ambitious

★ Think creatively

★ Are fearless

★ Problem solvers

★ High self-initiative

★ Understand basic finance principles

Entrepreneurship, on the other hand, is the point at which a person who has a thought follows up on that thought, typically to disturb the ongoing business sector with another item or administration. Business normally begins as a private venture, yet the drawn-out vision is a lot more noteworthy: to look for high benefits and catch a piece of the pie with a creative, groundbreaking thought.

At the centre, entrepreneurs are people who start businesses. However, on a more profound level, they're individuals who enhance. Somebody who begins a business is OK with inconvenience and stretching beyond their usual range of familiarity. They see difficulties and consider inventive ways of beating them. They fill society with groundbreaking thoughts and continue to invigorate the old ones.

The entrepreneurial mindset is a bunch of abilities that permit people to distinguish and capitalize on open doors, gain from their disappointments, and find lasting success regardless of the difficulties confronted. Research shows that a pioneering outlook is profoundly sought after by future managers, can work on scholastic outcomes, and is fundamental for making new business thoughts.

Turning into an effective entrepreneur begins with bringing an innovative outlook to your undertaking. The innovative mentality is a bunch of abilities, convictions, and perspectives you can bring to the undertaking of building another business. The fundamental components of this mentality are:

★ *Interest:*

A powerful entrepreneur questions everything, realizes everything they can, and is open to new and revolutionary thoughts, regardless of whether they go against their most essential suspicions.

★ *Freedom:*

There's no exact guide to progress as an entrepreneur. Transforming a groundbreaking thought into a fruitful business requires risk-taking and the capacity to design your best course of action without handholding from others.

★ *Strength:*

Prevailing as an entrepreneur means persevering through tension and disappointment yet additionally gaining and developing from those encounters.

★ *Convincingness:*

To fund-raise and develop their group, a hopeful entrepreneur should have the option to certainly offer their business thought to what is often a doubtful crowd.

★ *Center around helping other people:*

Entrepreneurs earn esteem by tackling issues for individuals around them. The best business visionaries are centered around making a positive impact instead of bringing in cash.

TYPES OF ENTREPRENEURSHIP

Entrepreneurship comes in many forms, whether they long to work for themselves or upset the state of affairs. Here are a few normal kinds of self-starters you could run into:

1. The creator:

This individual needs to do the following: understand the situation, envision items or business thoughts that don't yet exist, and attempt to bring them into the real world.

2. The small-scale business owners:

Private venture business visionaries utilize under 500 specialists. These individuals work in everything from little consultancies to famous neighborhood cafés. They grasp the worth of difficult work and drive a capable group of representatives.

3. Internet-based entrepreneurs:

Whether it's a second job or an everyday job, these business people make the Web work for them. They could sell items on Etsy, keep a famous monetary blog, or foster programming to convey on the web. In any case, they have an immediate relationship with clients through their web-based business.

4. The home-based business owners:

These individuals use their homes as their headquarters. A family plumbing business could utilize its home carport to store gear. Then again, a craftsman cleanser creator could use the storm cellar as their creation line. These individuals make their space work for them.

ADVANTAGES AND DISADVANTAGES OF ENTREPRENEURSHIP

While hopeful entrepreneurs can possibly procure monstrous distinction and fortune by beginning an effective business, entrepreneurship isn't without its difficulties. Below are some of the benefits and downsides.

Benefits of entrepreneurship

1. Work adaptability:

Entrepreneur implies independent work, which accompanies the capacity to set your own timetable and work where you need.

2. Capacity to follow your enthusiasm:

In the event that your imaginative thought is connected with your interests or leisure activities, an entrepreneur empowers you to make a vocation out of what you love.

3. Complete control:

Since they own their own organizations, business people have unlimited authority over their enterprising endeavors and the capacity to rapidly decide.

4. Inventiveness:

Without the weight of organization normal in enormous, mature organizations, business people can tackle issues imaginatively and try frequently.

5. Limitless acquisition potential:

As renowned business people like Imprint Zuckerberg or Bill Gates show, a startup entrepreneur with a fruitful business idea can make millions or even billions of dollars.

Downsides of Entrepreneurship

1. Monetary gamble:

Turning into an entrepreneur implies risking cash for your thoughts. In the event that it doesn't end up working, you'll be liable for managing disheartened financial backers and extraordinary bank credits.

2. Extended periods of time:

Between conceptualizing novel thoughts, charming likely financial backers, and dealing with the everyday tasks of their organizations, numerous business people work long and hard to make their fantasy a reality.

3. More noteworthy obligations:

As the head of your own business, everybody will be seeking your vision and course, which can cause colossal individual pressure.

4. High rivalry:

Since your business idea is creative, that doesn't mean you won't confront fierce opposition, whether from laid-out firms in your industry or different business people hoping to beat you to the end goal.

5. Temperamental pay:

While fruitful entrepreneurs might see a major payday, it will not work out more or less by accident. Meanwhile, expect lean times as you put all of your effort into developing your business.

CHAPTER TWO

THE ROLE OF AN ENTREPRENEUR

Entrepreneurs assume a critical role in any economy, utilizing the abilities and drive necessary to anticipate needs and offer groundbreaking thoughts for sale to the public. Entrepreneurship that ends up finding success in facing the dangers and challenges of making a startup is compensated with benefits and valuable learning experiences.

Entrepreneurship is one of the assets market analysts classify as necessary to creation, the other three being land or regular assets, work, and capital.

They ordinarily make a marketable strategy, employ work, get assets and support, and give initiative and the executives to the business.

Role of Entrepreneur in Society

The following are a few different ways that entrepreneurs assume a significant role in the public eye. Allow us to figure out more about them.

1. Entrepreneurs are Trailblazers

Innovation is rapidly changing the texture of each and every country's labor force. Old, common blue-collar positions are diminishing, and different occupations don't exist any longer. For instance, phone switchboard administrators, film projectionists, or lift chaperons

Entrepreneurs notice such changes and move toward making up for the shortfalls. They additionally notice the unfortunate results and misfortunes of certain occupations brought about by innovation. Notwithstanding, they sense open doors in the new scene. Subsequently, entrepreneurs develop. They make new items and administrations with propels in innovation that make prospects.

2. Entrepreneurs Make Occupations

As entrepreneurs start new organizations, they need to select workers. These new organizations become motors of occupation creation. As per the Private Venture Organization, little organizations have made 65% of new positions since the downturn.

Entrepreneurs create completely new enterprises and open doors for work. Suppose a football trainer is in Colorado. It was seen that youthful competitors accepted their instruction when they were on the training field; nonetheless, after they left, they got literally nothing. In this way, he did a business that gathered recordings for sports preparation and put them on a site.

Subsequently, presently hopeful competitors can get proficient directions and practice whenever and wherever the timing is ideal. This organization currently has in excess of 450 representatives in the United States of America and six other unfamiliar nations. None of these positions existed before this mentor in Colorado began its business.

3. Entrepreneurs Increase Expectations of Living

Business is a method. Business people (entrepreneurs) notice a need in the commercial center and utilize their creative gifts to look for an answer. They start another business and enroll representatives. The laborers procure compensation, which they spend in the neighborhood economy. All of this creates abundance for the populace and increases the expectation of living for everyone.

Studies from financial specialists show that efficiency increments work on the way of life for a populace. The strategy of a business venture prompts greater efficiency. Development applies more proficient advances to make a genuinely new thing, imaginative, or reach the next level. It tracks down additional optimal approaches to following through with something.

Accordingly, representatives become more effective. Benefits go up, and costs go down. Earnings rise, and companies request increments. All in all, the economy gets more grounded, taking many positions.

4. Entrepreneurship makes financial development possible.

It is critical to know how entrepreneurs add to the economy.

Beginning with new organizations creating abundance for the populace, new business sectors add abundance to the economy when business people put away their own cash to make inventive items and services. Banks and different financial backers offer more money to the new dares to give more assets at work.

Organizations pay charges on their benefits, and later, workers pay charges on their compensation. The public authority takes this money and spends it to animate the economy.

The GDP is a measure of a country's monetary status and improvement. A solid economy expands the total national output per capita of the country. Further developing GDP is a vital objective for financial improvement in light of the fact that every individual is turning out to be more useful and bringing in more cash.

5. Entrepreneurs change the Local area

Entrepreneurs assume a significant role locally. A business started by an entrepreneur has a major effect on the nearby local area. The new organization makes greater work by recruiting representatives who spend their pay in nearby stores, doing more business for those proprietors. The outcome of one business gains the headway of different associations.

Suppose the new business needs capable, instructed representatives with explicit abilities. A people group might answer by making specialized preparation schools and understudy programs that give these labourers. Everybody benefits. The organization gets the specialists it needs, and the local area gets a more qualified, educated populace with higher livelihoods.

The Job of Entrepreneurship in Business

Entrepreneurship is the most common way of making and maintaining another undertaking to create benefits. It is a pivotal calculation driving monetary development and improvement in both industrial and non-industrial nations. The pioneering movement makes new positions, encourages development, and drives market competition, which eventually helps customers.

The role of entrepreneurship in business couldn't possibly be more significant.

In this section, we will analyze the manner in which entrepreneurship contributes to financial development and improvement and investigate its different advantages.

Here are some of the contribution of entrepreneurship to business development

1. Increasing the expectation of living

One of the main advantages of entrepreneurship in monetary terms is that it increases the standard of living. By creating new organizations and occupations, entrepreneurship works on personal satisfaction for two people and networks, empowering ways for abundance creation.

Entrepreneurship upgrades employability, which thus drives financial seriousness. The outcome is better items and administrations, and eventually, more joyful purchasers.

2. Formation of New Positions

Entrepreneurship is a critical cause of occupation creation. By beginning new organizations, entrepreneurs open doors for themselves and others. This assists with lessening joblessness rates and further developing the general financial prosperity of the local area.

As indicated by the Worldwide Business Screen, entrepreneurship is responsible for making a great many positions around the world. This is especially significant in non-industrial nations, where work creation is basic for monetary development and destitution decreases.

3. Assists with killing Neediness In Neighborhoods

Entrepreneurship can assist with wiping out destitution in neighborhoods. By creating new organizations and occupations, businesses give individuals chances to advance their monetary circumstances.

This is especially significant in agricultural nations, where destitution is frequently far and wide. Entrepreneurship provides a method for people to further develop their monetary prosperity, which can at last prompt social change and general improvement.

4. Assists With People group Advancement

Entrepreneurship is significant as it likewise assumes a basic role in local area improvement. By creating new organizations, business people add to the monetary imperative of their networks. This can prompt expanded interest locally, which can bring about better foundations, administrations, and conveniences.

Entrepreneurship can likewise assist with encouraging a feeling of local area pride and proprietorship, which can contribute to the general improvement of the local area.

5. Gives Financial Autonomy

Entrepreneurship gives financial autonomy to people, towns, and nations. By creating new organizations, business people can create jobs and contribute to the general financial prosperity of their local area. This is especially significant for non-industrial nations, where financial power is often gathered in the possession of a couple of enormous companies.

Entrepreneurship gives an open door to people and private companies to contend on the lookout, which can prompt expanded monetary variety and steadiness.

6. Advantages Of New businesses Entering the Market

New businesses entering the market drive advancement and intensity. They challenge existing organizations to work on their items and administrations, which at last advantages purchasers.

The significance of new businesses couldn't possibly be more significant since they give new positions potential open doors and contribute to general financial development. They are fundamental for establishing a dynamic and lively business climate, which encourages development. Without new participants, existing firms aren't spurred to develop and can increase costs due to the enormous scope of syndication in the business.

7. Supports Capital Speculation

Entrepreneurship energizes capital interest in the two urban communities and nations. By making new organizations, entrepreneurs draw in ventures from both neighborhood and unfamiliar sources. This might actually open their capacity to get to various work markets and even enter unfamiliar business sectors sometime later.

This venture can add to the general monetary development of the local area as well as open new doors to business people and occupation seekers. Capital development is fundamental for establishing a manageable and flourishing business climate.

8. New Contestants Drive Market Advancement

Creative entrepreneurship is the main thrust behind market advancement. Entrepreneurs are known for their capacity to recognize holes on the lookout and concoct answers to fill those holes. This benefits the entrepreneur as well as the whole economy.

By zeroing in on business advancement, like growing new arrangements, items, or benefits, or working on existing ones, business people increase competition, prompting a diminution in costs and an expansion in quality.

In addition, creative business people are likewise responsible for minimizing expenses, which helps the general economy. By presenting new and more effective creation strategies, business visionaries can diminish the expense of creation. This prompts an expansion in supply, which thus prompts an expansion in sending out. This is especially significant for non-industrial nations that depend intensely on trade for their financial development.

9. Ideal Utilization of Assets

Entrepreneurs are additionally responsible for the ideal utilization of assets. By distinguishing new business opportunities and presenting new creation techniques, business visionaries can create more productive frameworks for using assets. This benefits the entrepreneur as well as the whole economy, as it prompts a decrease in squandering and an expansion in efficiency.

Moreover, business can likewise prompt the formation of new business sectors. By presenting new items or administrations, business visionaries can drive interest where none existed previously. This can prompt the advancement of completely new ventures, which can additionally contribute to the general improvement of the economy.

10. Expands Per Capita Pay (PCI) and Gross Public Item (GNP)

Entrepreneurship is a vital driver of financial development and improvement. By creating new organizations and occupations, business prompts an expansion in gross public goods and per capita pay. This is especially significant for emerging nations, where destitution and joblessness are significant issues.

As a matter of fact, studies have shown that the pioneering movement is emphatically connected with financial development. As per the European Exploration on Administration and Business Financial Matters, nations with elevated degrees of pioneering movement will generally have higher paces of monetary development.

In addition, entrepreneurship likewise assumes a significant role in advancing the adjusted provincial turn of events. By making new organizations and opening positions in regions that were recently immature, entrepreneurship can assist with diminishing provincial aberrations and advance through a large turn of events.

CHAPTER THREE

BUILDING AN EMPIRE: FROM DREAM TO REALITY

Building a business empire is definitely not a simple interaction. Frequently, it requires long periods of difficult work, tolerance, and a considerable measure of luck. Today, we'll take a gander at all that you really want to be aware of to boost your odds of coming out on top.

ENTREPRENEURSHIP FINANCING

We cannot talk about building a domain in entrepreneurship without talking about financing the business. Given the riskiness of new business, the securing of capital subsidizing is especially difficult, and numerous entrepreneurs manage it by means of bootstrapping: funding a business utilizing techniques such as, for example, utilizing their own cash, giving perspiration value to decrease work costs, limiting stock, and calculating receivables.

While certain entrepreneurs are solitary players attempting to get independent companies going on a tight budget, others take on accomplices furnished with more noteworthy access to capital and different assets. In these circumstances, new firms might get support from financial speculators, private backers, mutual funds, crowdfunding, or through additional conventional sources, for example, bank advances.

RESOURCES FOR ENTREPRENEURS

There are an assortment of supporting assets for entrepreneurs beginning their own business.

Acquiring independent venture credit through the Small Business Administration (SBA) can assist entrepreneurs with getting their businesses going with reasonable credit. Here, the SBA associates organizations to advance suppliers.

On the off chance that entrepreneurs will surrender a piece of value in their business, then they might track down funding as private backers and financial speculators. These kinds of financial backers likewise provide direction, mentorship, and associations, notwithstanding capital.

Crowdfunding has likewise turned into a famous way for entrepreneurs to raise capital, especially through Kickstarter or Indiegogo. Along these lines, an entrepreneur makes a page for their item and a financial objective to reach while promising certain givebacks to the individuals who give, like items or encounters.

BOOTSTRAPPING FOR ENTREPRENEURS

Bootstrapping alludes to building an organization exclusively from your reserve funds as an entrepreneur as well as from the underlying deals produced using your business. This is a troublesome interaction, as everything in the monetary gamble is put on the entrepreneur, and there is no place for blunder. Assuming that the business falls flat, the entrepreneur likewise may lose all of their life reserve funds.

The benefit of bootstrapping is that an entrepreneur can maintain the business with their own vision and no external obstruction or financial backers requesting easy gains. That being said, once in a while, having an untouchable's help can help a business as opposed to hurting it. Many organizations have prevailed with a bootstrapping technique; however, it is a troublesome way.

Assemble a Domain: Picking The Right Starting points for Your Business Domain

We should begin with the fundamentals.

What is a Business Domain?

A business domain doesn't have a firm definition. It is frequently connected with extravagant organizations with branches laid out from one side of the planet to the other. In any case, this isn't the main way it may be characterized.

Instructions to construct a domain

There is no norm, and there are no boundaries or edges after which the business transforms into a domain. A business domain is any business that begins without any preparation, shows what it can do, and keeps on developing after some time.

For instance, you could work in one city; however, on the off chance that you have two or three branches and you have the market nailed down, the vast majority would consider this a business realm. Like a genuine domain, a business realm is tied to having control in your industry

Fabricate a Business Domain: How to Get everything rolling

A solid beginning is significant for settling a business and provides the business with the right guidance for improvement. To assemble a domain, an entrepreneur should be everything except unconstrained.

Each step of the accompanying document takes research and careful examination to be executed appropriately and satisfy its motivation.

★ Offer What Individuals Need

Concluding which item you need to sell is the initial step to building a business domain.

Having confidence in a particular item is perfect, yet it isn't sufficient. Choosing an item that you respect, or one that you have a positive sentiment about, isn't an assurance that it will create gain.

Concentrating available and situating your item perfectly is critical prior to choosing an item. Redoing an item founded on available requirements is more productive than pursuing the direction.

While the pattern might bring you prompt achievement, an item fabricated in view of a technique will have more achievement and steadiness over the long haul. Moreover, the most common way of picking an item to sell or make ought to be as unambiguous as could be expected, particularly when you are beginning.

Zeroing in on one item, yet additionally a particular specialty of an item, makes the cycle obvious and quantifiable. This makes it more straightforward to bring up the shortcomings and alter the cycle likewise, as well as restrict any monetary misfortune.

Additionally, it's vital to offer quality items to excel. For instance, in only a couple of years, Cheerful Houseplants has laid a good foundation for itself as one of the top indoor plant stores in the UK. How? With difficult work loading quality items.

★ Learn and Procure

Another important step that ought to be taken before sending off an item is learning. Learning includes concentrating on everything connected with the business:

- The creation interaction,
- The monetary perspective,
- The buyer conducts
- And any remaining small subtleties.

Building a business domain implies being the most incredible in your industry. This is essentially unimaginable on the off chance that you don't know basically everything there is to know about your specialty.

★ Research the Market

To construct a domain around an item or a help, it quickly sets you in the place of "the master."

In this way, you ought to be very well informed about the business to make it look valid.

Additionally, the more you know, the simpler it is to try not to be deceived or succumb to misrepresentation because of naiveté. It is savvy to invest sufficient energy in learning and exploring; it isn't burned through to know that this time.

One method for beginning your business domain is to detect a hole on the lookout. Consider how

Mac cornered the market for tablet PCs when they delivered the iPad—something the world had never seen and didn't understand they required.

The time you spend learning will be converted into cash you will procure later.

★ Tracking down a mentor

Business advisors are likewise a choice that could be so valuable, particularly in deeply grounded enterprises. An extraordinary assistance is causing companions and building associations with individuals who have been down this street previously.

There is always somebody's experience that you can learn from. Also, this will be of extraordinary assistance later on in the event that you want an accomplice, or participation with a contender.

At the point when you begin to develop your business realm, you will experience issues that not many individuals will comprehend. It is vital to Have a specialist guide.

- Enlist a mentor for your business realm details
- Recruiting a mentor can prompt significantly better results.
- Listening is a component of the examination cycle that is worried about getting to realize your shoppers better.
a. What are their concerns with different brands in that industry?
b. What do they need?
c. How might you work on their experience?

d. Which sort of administration or item do they require?

Furthermore, obviously, what might cause them to supplant the brand they are faithful to with another?

The best spot to figure out additional information about purchasers, is to ask these shoppers themselves.

★ Center around Acquiring Money

While beginning a business, things can undoubtedly appear to be overwhelming, as there are numerous things to get ready and finish. Cash is the soul of business and is fundamental to supporting its progression and development.

Unfortunate income is one of the main sources of business disappointment.

For administration based organizations, the best model would make all installments front and center to be in charge of your income. Stores are likewise a decent choice to get what is going on and keep away from cash holes.

In any event, for retail, you can give a direct-front, regularly scheduled installment framework as a trade-off for advantages like free conveyance or limited costs. This is particularly significant for items which purchasers purchase on a recurrent premise.

This assists you with arranging your month-to-month focus ahead and keeping away from the hole between when you get cash and your monetary responsibilities like staff pay rates or stock.

★ Minimize Expenses

Obviously, if you construct a realm for the future, it won't begin as one. Nearly everybody begins with a limited spending plan, either to limit risk or because of absence of assets.

With regards to office space, showcasing, and framework, you ought to stay away from retail, however much could be expected.

There are more business costs than we regularly expect. Office space, furniture and recording frameworks, telephones, stock, office adornments, and publicizing are things that have numerous other options.

Recollect that on the off chance that your costs are high, in any event, making an enormous income won't protect your realm. Thus, give your all to finding the best arrangements; this will definitely affect your business.

★ Misjudge Costs and Underrate Incomes

A brilliant rule for at whatever point you are setting up a technique, a spending plan, or any venture plan: anticipate the least pay and the most extreme costs.

This isn't tied in with having a worse viewpoint, by any stretch of the imagination. To fabricate a realm, you must be cautious with cash matters since it is delicate when a business is still in its underlying stage.

Building your essential financial plan in view of the most dire outcome imaginable is tied in with getting ready for any test your organization might confront.

Over the long haul, you will have a more clear vision of your assessed pay and costs, and it will be a lot simpler to plan.

Instructions to assemble a domain capital

Income can represent the moment of truth for another business.

★ Deals and Promoting

A significant number of the people who fabricate a domain start by zeroing in on building a brand picture and burn through much cash in light of this objective. Obviously, building serious areas of strength for a picture is an unquestionable requirement for any extraordinary business.

Nonetheless, it isn't something that one ought to begin with.

Building a brand comes after laying out the business on firm ground. Deals and showcasing for your newly conceived business domain ought to have one objective: getting leads. Every one of your endeavors, monetary or not, ought to be worried about getting clients.

Make a showcase and deal channel framework that you can work with, test, and measure. Like that, you settle your business with income and then construct your image as one that is now respectable.

Instructions to Assemble a Domain: The 3 Stages that Come After the Beginning

So whenever you've laid out your business, the subsequent stage is to develop it into a completely fledged domain. Scaling your business brings a totally different arrangement of difficulties. The following are three stages you can take from the beginning to get your business realm in a good position:

★ Construct Frameworks

Assuming you think robotization is costly, have a go at doing things physically. Robotization is a gigantic life hack.

Maintaining a business empire could overpower It requires investment to fabricate a domain. Frequently, you will set aside yourself, squandering opportunity and assets on exercises that do not affect you at all. Dispose of that by doling out these errands within a framework.

Assuming you are paying somebody to finish assignments that a robotization device can deal with better, you are heading down an unacceptable path. The right situation will be the foundation of your business, and it will assist with saving your most significant resource, time.

Precision is something different that makes setting up a framework an unquestionable necessity in each association. A business domain ought to be proficient, truly. Mistakes are unsuitable, particularly today, in a culture where clients have the best standards.

Bringing down your blunder rate is fundamental to introducing your business as a strong substance.

★ Employ the Ideal Public

Generally speaking, entrepreneurs start all alone, or with an accomplice or two, and no more. Then, at that point, they spend the main period of their business doing everything themselves, from tidying up the workplace to bookkeeping and promoting, and everything in between.

This might be effective for times when you actually can't stand to enlist individuals. When your business has endured that stage, don't allow it to wait.

Move to the next stage by recruiting individuals to help you. You will have some trouble giving over undertakings since you are accustomed to finishing everything the manner in which you need it.

Notwithstanding, you will be astonished at how much the cycle will be quicker and significantly more financially fulfilling.

It's a given that prior to beginning anything, you ought to employ legitimate guidance and a bookkeeper, then, at that point, recruit more assets as you go as per the idea of your business. Recall that you can never fabricate a domain alone.

Sooner or later, you'll likewise need to recruit a promoter to assist with scaling your business.

★ Extend and Scale Reasonably

Numerous business visionaries wonder whether or not to make a stride that includes development. At the point when a business passes its most memorable stage and starts developing, business people feel good and less fretted over whether their business will bring in cash.

In this manner, choosing to grow turns into a stage beyond the business' usual range of familiarity. Development could be additional help, another product offering, or another branch opening. Everything requires recruiting new assets, extra costs, arranging, time, and exertion.

Obviously, extension incorporates some risk; nevertheless, it is a significant step that each business realm should go through.

Knowing when to grow is vital to supporting a steady domain. Furthermore, paying attention to the criticism of your clients and contrasting your situation with rivals in the market are two fundamental factors that you ought to consider prior to growing.

Realms are not intended to be little new businesses until the end of time. They work to be perfect and drive ventures.

Normal entrepreneurial prerequisites to develop a domain

Starting up as a hopeful entrepreneur, by and large, requires:

- A business thought (which includes a thing, organization, process, or new development)
- Individuals to help the work, whether as representatives, merchants, or guides
- A cycle by which the item or administration will be conveyed, or the innovation will be created
- Enough subsidizing to help the improvement of the plan to the point that it produces income
- A companion survey strategy

In taking into account what sort of business to begin, survey:

- *Your inclinations:* Are any of your interests, leisure activities, or interests ready for development?

- *Your experience and encounters:* How has your own set of experiences set you up for the difficulties of being an entrepreneur

- *Your monetary assets:* Might you at any point accumulate the essential assets to get a given business thought going?

- Neglected market needs: What business potential open doors exist in your picked industry or field?

- Issues you can settle: What difficulties do your abilities and information set you up to address in your outer climate?

- Your organization and associations: Which individuals in your expert organization assist you in your business with venturing?

What are the characteristics of a fruitful Entrepreneur?

Beginning another business accompanies an innate measure of hazard. You can do all that right, yet outside occasions could prompt an adverse result. While there's no recipe for business venture, there are positive or negative business person attributes.

Here are a few abilities you really want to turn into an effective business person:

1. Discipline

The main characteristic of an entrepreneur is self-control. You want to accomplish the work — in any event, when you don't feel like it.

On the off chance that you have normal everyday employment, this could mean working extended periods of time. You'll need the self-inspiration to get up ahead of schedule or stay awake until late as you start your new pursuit.

2. Interest

The best business visionaries generally need to find out more. They pose great inquiries and search for amazing chances to develop themselves and their businesses. These individuals don't harp on what they assume they know; however, all things considered, they change their perspectives when given new data.

Their interest in learning is simply aspect of how they approach the world.

3. Innovativeness

The fact that it drives numerous fruitful new businesses makes this a flash. Innovativeness isn't only for creatives; it's an expertise that everybody can develop. Business people generally search for inventive ways of taking care of issues or conveying help, frequently with restricted assets.

They search in a wide range of spots for motivation, and their imagination helps fuel their adoration for what they are doing. Find what gives you thoughts and use it as your fuel.

To develop this ability, rely on propensities that foster innovation. It very well may be music, contemplation, or meeting new individuals.

4. Eagerness to attempt things

As a business visionary, you'll continually be given new errands that challenge your range of abilities. Cleverness remains inseparable from trial and error and critical thinking. Be prepared to get imaginative, break new ground, and pull from your huge organization, encounters, and abilities to take on a test.

Plan to watch your answer come up short as well. It's unavoidable, and each disappointment is a chance to learn and develop your thoughts.

If you plan well and frame measurements for the following achievement, you can rapidly make changes and track down fitting arrangements.

Show your item to a trusted gathering of companions, read statistical surveying to check whether there's sufficient interest, and keep up-to-date on the most recent industry news.

These systems will assist you in proceeding with carefully weighed-out courses of action while attempting new things.

5. Trustworthiness

In the business world, you're trustworthy only so far as your actions justify it. Trustworthiness and uprightness are significant attributes of a business visionary. These character attributes will receive a few rewards:

- You will foster a standing as areas of strength for a legitimate communicator
- Your representatives will respect your initiative

- Clients will realize you can follow through on your commitments
- Individuals will be more able to loan you cash for your next thought
- Your people group will uphold you during difficult stretches

6. Continuously have an arrangement

Effective organizations take risks with minimal effort. They look far into the future, with fallbacks to adjust to surprising occasions.

You ought to have a dream for your organization 5–10 years from now.

To rejuvenate that vision, you can utilize the Brilliant Objective Setting technique to set short- and long-term business objectives.

These are objectives that are:

- ***Explicit:*** What is the specific result you're expecting?
- ***Quantifiable:*** How might you realize you accomplished this result?
- ***Attainable:*** Is it sensible for you to hope to accomplish this objective?
- ***Reasonable:*** Might you at any point show up at your objective with your ongoing assets?
- ***Time-Bound:*** Do you have a reasonable cutoff time for your objective?

Every objective ought to expand on the last, carrying you nearer to your vision and nearer to the real world. Likewise, recall that a ton can change throughout the long term. You're permitted to change your arrangement if necessary.

7. Grasping the worth of taking care of oneself

Incredible pioneers comprehend that depletion and exhaustion are catastrophes waiting to happen. They might have every one of the abilities on the planet. Be that as it may, without appropriate wellbeing, they will not have the option to execute. Planning time for taking care of oneself will repay you ten times.

A similar way of thinking applies to your workers. Ensure they figure out the worth of their work and urge them to rest when they need it. They will repay you with an uplifting outlook and a more grounded, hard-working attitude.

8. Facing challenges

Daring individuals frequently as well as business pioneers. In any case, you ought to be sure about your methodology and have a plan B all set should things turn out badly.

This is a trait of a decent business visionary since entrepreneurs frequently need to go outside of what might be expected. This can be unnerving, yet business people should save their apprehensions and take the leap expected to make their vision show some signs of life.

9. Versatility

The world is continually changing, as is the manner in which we carry on with work. Entrepreneurs have no deficiency of startling difficulties and shock valuable open doors, so they should act rapidly and proficiently.

This versatility makes a business fruitful, and it's especially valid for business people with a Millennial labor force. As opposed to attempting to drive formats that worked previously, business people should be adaptable to changing standards like half-breed work models and offer a better representative balance between serious and fun activities.

10. Tirelessness after disappointment

Effective entrepreneurs comprehend that disappointment isn't the apocalypse. All things being equal, disappointment is a practice for progress. Continuing, notwithstanding any detours, expands your certainty, conviction, innovativeness, and advancement.

In the event that you fizzle, you learn illustrations to apply to the following test and show yourself that you're grittier than you naturally suspected. All that extreme reasoning might prompt revolutionary outcomes.

Normal errors to stay away from as an entrepreneur

It's not difficult to commit errors in the event that this is your most memorable time sending off a business, yet perhaps we can assist you with staying away from a couple. The following are things to really focus on:

1. Not adhering to your spending plan

It's not difficult to get out of hand when you're beginning. Be mindful so as not to blow your spending plan excessively fast. Adhere to the basics for the time being, such as recruiting the right staff, and putting resources into the right apparatus, and working out your client list. The rest will come later.

2. Going with misguided recruiting choices

Your business will flourish or kick the bucket, depending on who you recruit. Pick your representatives carefully. Search for individuals who share your pioneering mentality and have experience working at another business.

It's likewise valuable to find individuals who have unexpected mastery in comparison to you to cover any of your vulnerable sides. In the event that you believe you're group could benefit from a workable pace, you should consider furnishing them with business training.

3. Laying out impossible objectives

Try not to hope to make the NASDAQ in your most memorable year. Put forth reachable objectives while you're beginning. Stick to the shrewd technique we framed previously.

4. Neglecting to designate

You recruited incredible individuals. Use them! Numerous business visionaries don't have the foggiest idea how to delegate to other people, or they're hesitant to. Consider whether you really want to run an errand. You have no control over everything, so just keep the main ones.

Allocate errands in light of others' assets, set clear assumptions, and check in with them consistently. They're your group, and they will convey.

5. Pursuing choices out of dread

Clear your head prior to pursuing large choices. Feelings like apprehension, outrage, or dissatisfaction can cloud your judgment.

At the point when you experience what is happening, make a stride back, be aware of your sentiments, and move toward the issue later with an unmistakable psyche.

WORK ON YOUR INNOVATIVE ABILITIES

Current pioneers need an inexorably long list of administrative abilities. This is the thing you ought to chip away at as you foster your business:

- Enticement
- Critical thinking

- Relational abilities

- Adaptability

- Self-inspiration

- Organizing

- Undivided attention

CHAPTER FOUR

RISK MANAGEMENT IN ENTREPRENEURSHIP

In the fast-moving universe of business, taking risks is an urgent component that can represent the deciding moment for a business. Effective business visionaries comprehend the significance of embracing risk and settling on determined choices that move their endeavors forward.

Risk-taking in entrepreneurship implies venturing outside one's usual range of familiarity, rocking the boat, and quickly jumping all over chances that others might avoid.

In this section, we will dive into the idea of chance taking in entrepreneurship (likewise alluded to as gamble with the board), investigate various kinds of dangers looked at by entrepreneurs, feature the meaning of hazard taking in pioneering achievement, give instances of hazard taking business visionaries, and look at the potential dangers implied in being a business visionary.

WHAT IS RISK-TAKING IN ENTREPRENEURSHIP?

Risk-taking in entrepreneurship alludes to the readiness and capacity of business visionaries to decide and make moves that include vulnerability, expected misfortune, and the chance of disappointment.

It is an innate piece of the enterprising excursion as entrepreneurs explore unfamiliar domains, improve, and take a stab at development. Risk-taking in business implies dissecting expected chances, evaluating their likely effect, and proceeding with reasonable plans of action that offer a good gamble-reward proportion. All things considered, most potential open doors have a component of hazard when they're sought after.

SORTS OF RISKS IN ENTREPRENEURSHIP

As an entrepreneur, it's critical that you're ready, proficient, and don't face risky challenges.

Each chance you take ought to be painstakingly surveyed. Along these lines, you'll have the option to dispassionately compute the sort and level of hazard implied to guarantee the return on initial capital investment merits the work and possible result of disappointment.

★ Monetary Gamble

A monetary gamble is a typical kind of hazard looked at by entrepreneurs. It includes the possible loss of venture or monetary assets because of business disappointments, market changes, or unanticipated conditions. Business visionaries frequently contribute their own capital or look for external subsidies to begin or develop their endeavors, exposing themselves to monetary dangers. Overseeing income, getting support, and checking costs are fundamental parts of relieving monetary gambles.

★ Market Hazard

Market risk connects with the vulnerabilities related to the interest in an item or administration on the lookout. Business visionaries should evaluate economic situations, shopper inclinations, serious scenes, and potential changes that could influence their business. Market gamblers remember changes in purchaser conduct, changes in innovation, financial slumps, or problematic developments. Remaining informed about market patterns, directing statistical surveying, and adjusting techniques in like manner can assist with overseeing market chances.

★ Functional Gamble

Functional gamble relates to difficulties and vulnerabilities experienced in everyday business activities. It incorporates dangers, for example, inventory network disturbances, creation issues, administrative consistency, ability obtaining and maintenance, and innovative disappointments. Business people should recognize and alleviate functional dangers to guarantee smooth business tasks. Executing successful cycles, directing gamble appraisals, and laying out alternate courses of action are essential for overseeing functional dangers.

★ Reputational Chance

Reputational risk implies the possible damage to an organization's image or reputation because of negative exposure, unfortunate client encounters, deceptive ways of behaving, legal issues, or item disappointments. Business visionaries should be aware of their activities, keep up with straightforwardness, and focus on consumer loyalty to moderate reputational gambles. Building major areas of strength for a company, conveying quality items or administrations, and effectively overseeing client connections are vital to limiting reputational gambles.

★ Business Hazard

A business that takes excessively high risks while sending off another item or going into another market might possibly endanger its own reality if overutilized. This implies that it's own representative's might try to lose their positions, which would at last influence their own families and lives. In this manner, it's critical that facing challenges in business is thought about cautiously.

★ Work-Life Unevenness

Maintaining a business calls for huge investment and exertion, frequently bringing about work-life irregularities for entrepreneurs. The strain to succeed, long working hours, and steady independent direction can negatively affect individual connections and prosperity. It is critical for business people to focus on taking care of themselves, put down stopping points, and run representative errands to keep a solid balance between fun and serious activities.

★ Vulnerability and Stress

Entrepreneurship is intrinsically dubious, and business people should work in a climate where results are not ensured. The pressure of overseeing chances, settling on pivotal choices, and managing unanticipated hindrances can overpower. Entrepreneurs should foster compelling pressure methods, fabricate an encouraging group of people, and develop flexibility to explore through testing times.

★ Feeling of dread toward Disappointment

The feeling of dread toward disappointment can be a critical mental boundary for entrepreneurs. The potential for business mishaps or not living up to assumptions can prompt self-uncertainty and faltering. Beating the apprehension about disappointment is fundamental for business visionaries to proceed with reasonable plans of action, seek after imaginative thoughts, and keep a development-situated mentality.

THE IMPORTANCE OF RISK-TAKING IN ENTREPRENEURSHIP

To develop your business, you'll need to take some risk. In any case, why might you need to completely embrace the possibility that something startling may occur?

1. Driving Development and Development

Risk-taking is fundamental for driving development and encouraging business development. Business people who will take instructed business gambles frequently seek after groundbreaking thoughts, challenge customary reasoning, and upset existing business sectors. By embracing vulnerability and exploring different avenues regarding novel methodologies, business people can present imaginative items, administrations, and plans of action that resound with clients and move their dares to progress.

2. Acquiring Upper hand

Business visionaries who proceed with well-balanced plans of action frequently gain an upper hand on the lookout. By recognizing and seeking out open doors that others might disregard or consider excessively hazardous, business visionaries can separate themselves from contenders. Risk-taking permits business people to hold onto new business sectors, investigate undiscovered specialties, and position their organizations exceptionally, giving them an upper hand and expanding their possibilities of long-term achievement.

3. Learning and Versatility

Risk-taking in business provides important opportunities for growth. Regardless of whether an endeavor succeeds, the examples gained from facing challenges add to self-improvement and expert turn of events. Daring people foster strength, versatility, and critical thinking abilities, which are fundamental for exploring the difficulties of business and taking advantage of future chances. By embracing risk, business visionaries figure out how to oversee vulnerability, pursue informed choices, and change their procedures in view of market criticism and evolving conditions.

4. Beating the Apprehension about Disappointment

A feeling of dread toward disappointment is a typical mental boundary for entrepreneurs. Notwithstanding, facing challenges permits business people to stand up to and beat this apprehension. By recognizing that disappointment is plausible, business people can take on a development outlook and view disappointments as significant growth opportunities as opposed to unfavorable deterrents. Risk-taking assists business visionaries with building versatility, steadiness, and the capacity to quickly return from misfortunes, which are indispensable characteristics for long-term achievement.

The most effective method to further develop risk-taking in business venture

Everybody can further develop their gamble-taking attitude. Utilize these tips to impact the manner in which you ponder chance to work on your chances of achievement.

UTILIZE A GAMBLE EVALUATION STRUCTURE

Apply this helpful system to a gamble you experience as an entrepreneur.

1. Identify the dangers that your organization might confront.

2. Categorize the dangers in view of their qualities (e.g., item risk, market risk, and so on) and likely effects.

3. Select the potential techniques used to moderate the gamble (e.g., welcoming on a CTO, delivering a model to your main interest group, and so on).

4. Implement and test the potential relief method(s).

5. Assess the appropriateness of the moderation techniques.

6. Authorize the choice to face the gamble.

7. Monitor execution over the long run.

Following this deliberate cycle for surveying and assessing dangers will assist you in coming to brilliant conclusions about which opportunities to take and guarantee that you have relief methods set up.

★ Begin with more modest dangers

Not all dangers are equal. For example, choosing to investigate your business thoughts as a side gig implies less risk than recruiting your most memorable full-time worker.

On the off chance that you're simply beginning as a business visionary or haven't taken numerous business gambles previously, consider focusing on more modest open doors that are simpler or less exorbitant to investigate. Along these lines, you'll have the option to test and learn all the more often, without apprehension about critical misfortune.

★ Fabricate a culture where gestures of recognition and shrewd gamble-taking

Organization culture isn't only for laid-out organizations; entrepreneurs ought to be purposeful about what ways of behaving and needs are generally significant for their organization all along.

Consider including shrewd gamble-taking as a mainstay of your way of life, regardless of whether you're a solopreneur. Empower everybody (counting yourself) to take determined and all around contemplated risks.

CHAPTER FIVE

METHODS TO APPLY TO ACHIEVE SUCCESS IN ENTREPRENEURSHIP

Entrepreneurship can give you opportunity, abundance, and the capacity to construct your optimal way of life. However, there are also many difficulties in business that can impede you from accomplishing those objectives and even make business more troublesome than your past life.

In this chapter, we will be discussing four important methods to apply to achieve success in entrepreneurship. They are:

1. Overcoming difficulties
2. Advertising
3. Savings

4. Investing

OVERCOMING DIFFICULTIES

Throughout the long term, we'll frequently ask our crowd, "What are the difficulties of entrepreneurship?" and similar responses by and large come up. The following are six of the most widely recognized difficulties of business we've experienced throughout the long term and how to conquer them.

1. Collaboration and assignment:

A great many people get into business since they have specific expertise. They then, at that point, construct a business around getting compensated for that expertise. However, that isn't exactly a business, right? That is the very thing we would contemplate on an errand.

So one of the greatest difficulties of entrepreneurship is changing from that "work" to an "organization" that runs without help from anyone else and is at this point not reliant upon you. Furthermore, to do that, you really want a group, and you should have the option to delegate to them.

We've observed that there are two essential difficulties with collaboration and entrepreneurship.

The first is that business people get hung up on how they will follow through with something, and they hit a barrier when they don't have the capacity or resources to do it without any other individual's assistance.

The least demanding method for bypassing this is to use the basic idea of Who Not How. As opposed to asking, "How should I do this?", inquire, "Who can do this for me?"

At the point when you initially begin in business, you might need to do everything yourself. Yet, proportional and developed, you want to move away from that "how" mentality and take on a "who" outlook.

The next stage is recruiting great individuals and building a group that can assist you with accomplishing your business objectives.

Our most memorable suggestion is to eliminate "representative" from your vocabulary and supplant it with "colleague."

A worker is somebody who holds a task, while a colleague is an individual working in their special capacity (what they love to do endlessly best). There is a reasonable distinction between the two, and that is unquestionably essential to comprehend for anybody getting into entrepreneurship.

You likewise need to change your point of view while recruiting. Recruiting a colleague is certainly not a "cost"; it's an interest in your organization's future. At the point when you put resources into extraordinary colleagues, you make group multipliers that will thusly allow you gigantic profits from your venture. This can be hard for individuals new to entrepreneurship; it might appear to be a huge expense to recruit a group. However, what they don't understand is that they're getting a monstrous return.

Need to become familiar with this normal test of a business venture? Look at our collaboration and designation assets.

2. Concentration and efficiency:

Regardless of what industry you're in or what your plan of action is, the way to success in entrepreneurship is to remain fixed on the right things consistently.

At the point when we ask our crowd, "What are the difficulties of entrepreneurship?", one of the most popular reactions is constant fixation and effectiveness. Many individuals battle with this in entrepreneurship since they feel as though there's such a huge amount to do in their business. They don't feel like they're being sufficiently useful, or they can't zero in on one errand since there are such countless different difficulties consuming their brain.

One basic hint is to quit attempting to do 1,000,000 things consistently. Allot yourself three errands to run every day (ideally the prior night) and focus just on finishing those three things. When you complete them, you're free to either stop or continue onward. Whatever else you do is a reward.

This will simplify everything in your business and permit you to put your full spotlight on each test in turn. What we've found is that the vast majority wind up achieving more with this strategy in light of the fact that once they complete the initial three things on their list, they're empowered and prepared to continue onward.

We've nitty-gritty a lot more systems to battle this test of business in our sites, webcasts, and different assets on Concentration And Efficiency.

3. Balance between serious and fun activities:

The typical entrepreneur works 66 hours out of every week, and many work undeniably more than that. At the point when it seems like everything depends on you, it tends to be challenging to step away. This is one of the most incredibly upsetting difficulties of business, as it can cause burnout, influence your connections, and, surprisingly, be unsafe for your wellbeing.

Yet, actually staying at work past 40 hours doesn't work—particularly in entrepreneurship! Many individuals are under the suspicion that functioning longer and harder will get them to their objectives quicker. That is essentially false in entrepreneurship.

What we've found is that the more spare energy business visionaries have, the more imaginative they become. The more imaginative they become, the more fruitful they are with regards to income and benefit.

Working less yet being exceptionally vigorous and innovative while you're working really gives 10x more prominent outcomes. Try not to trust us. Look at the overpower and balance between fun and serious activities assets we have on this test. This has been demonstrated endlessly, time and again, explicitly regarding business.

To lay it out plainly, assuming that you feel like you're investing an excess of energy in your business, you presumably are! Recall why you embraced entrepreneurship in any case: opportunity!

4. Growing positive routines and accomplishing objectives:

There's a justification for why self-improvement and entrepreneurship are so interwoven. In a task, you can approach your everyday obligations, get advanced, and accomplish progress. In entrepreneurship, there are significantly more difficulties as there's no set path to follow.

To accomplish progress in your business, you want to set objectives and accomplish them. Doing that is more enthusiastic than it could sound! It's one of the most notable challenges of undertaking

In this way, here's a speedy tip from Dan Sullivan to foster beneficial routines that will assist you with accomplishing your objectives—either in business or some other piece of your life.

At the point when a great many people attempt to foster beneficial routines, they see what's happening in their lives at that point. All things being equal, look toward what's in store. Think 5, 10, or 25 years later and ask yourself, "What propensities could I need to begin today that I could in any case do a long time from now?"

This is an effective method for beginning new propensities that you will really keep all through your vocation in entrepreneurship. On the off chance that you can imagine yourself doing it a long time from now, it makes it more straightforward to begin.

Regardless, we ought to take it a step further. Ask yourself, "What penchants might the singular I at some point should be in about a year that I don't have?" and "What propensities could it merit doing consistently so I can move to the next level?"

These basic inquiries will grow your reasoning and assist you with creating propensities that are not difficult to begin, practical, and significant for your life and business.

Assuming that you're searching for more data on framing propensities, defining objectives, and making progress, look at our Objective Setting And Achievement Propensities assets. Framing positive routines is fundamental to beating the many difficulties of entrepreneurship.

5. Tarrying and using time effectively:

Numerous business visionaries battle with using time effectively, and one of the main drivers is stalling. At the point when you're compelled to do everything in your business yourself, there will unavoidably be exercises that you fear, which will make you dawdle.

What a great many people don't understand, in any case, is that tarrying is often a sign that greater things are coming, particularly with respect to business. We should investigate how that functions.

In the first place, record what you're delaying today. Then take a gander at your rundown and tell yourself, "I'm not doing these things since something greater is coming. What's the greater thing that is coming?"

The explanation a great many people hesitate — particularly in business — is on the grounds that they're focusing on exercises that aren't great for them or their business. These are exercises that don't use their Interesting skills and don't challenge them.

You know, where it counts, that there are far superior things you could be investing your time in. Carrying those far superior things to the front of your brain will create a rush of experiences and conceivable outcomes. You can then zero in on the greater, more significant activities while allowing others to deal with the errands you were fearing.

There are numerous different features of time usage in entrepreneurship. Assuming that you might want to study this normal test, look at our Time Usage assets.

6. Business development and scaling:

If you somehow happen to ask any irregular individual, "What are the difficulties of business venture?" Their cerebrum would probably default to growing a business.

Also, generally, they'd be correct. Sorting out some way to develop your business is the clearest and most overwhelming test of business. There are a huge number of ways to grow a business, and deciding what direction is best for you can feel like an unimaginable test.

At Vital Mentor, we aren't worried about low-down promoting strategies or "development hacks" that are so normal in the business venture space. All things considered, we assume the most effective way to develop your business is to grow your reasoning. Here is an illustration of one straightforward activity any business visionary can do to rapidly comprehend what they ought to zero in on to develop their business.

To begin with, distinguish every one of the ways in which you're bringing in cash into your business at the present time. Then, pose yourself the accompanying four inquiries for every income stream and grade your response on a scale of one to five:

> 1. If you stay with this movement, could it at any point go 10x?

2. Does this movement interest and persuade you?

3. Is this a movement that could last for the last 25 years?

4. Is this a movement that could introduce the chance of consistent new development?

Prevailing in entrepreneurship is in many cases more about inspiration, imagination, and development than showcasing contrivances and plans of action. By responding to these inquiries, you'll find one part of your business that inspires you, has the potential for development, and can give you consistent advancement for years to come. Multiplying down on that action will be the way to long term, predictable development.

ADVERTISING

Advertising in business is a kind of showcasing correspondence used to support, convince, or control a client to make or keep on taking some move. The ideal outcome is to drive shopper behavior as a business offering.

The essential job of publicizing is to illuminate potential clients regarding the items and services on the lookout and persuade them to make a purchase. Through commercials, clients are educated regarding new items, their jobs, their advantages, and the costs at which they are made accessible to them. It is a strategy used to impact individuals' brains and empower more deals.

The fundamental reason for publicizing is to convey the appropriate message to clients and planned clients. The motivation behind publicizing is to persuade clients that an organization's administrations or items are awesome, to improve the picture of the organization, bring up and make a requirement for their items or administrations, show new purposes for the laid out ones, declare new items and projects, build up the singular messages of the salesmen, attract clients to the business, and hold existing clients.

Promoting lies in the advancement portion of the advertising blend, yet it also applies to a wide range of various P's. Advancing one's business is vital to making one's business effective. Advancement, along with an extraordinary item, key situation, and a sensible cost, will assist an advertiser with working his way to the top. Advancing doesn't mean surrendering his publicizing to the informal exchange of his ongoing client.

Promoting gives an immediate line of communication to your current and planned clients about your item or administration. The reason for promoting is to:

- Make clients mindful of your item or administration.
- Persuade clients that your organization's item or administration is appropriate for their requirements.
- Make a longing for your item or administration.
- Upgrade the image of your organization.
- Report new items or administrations.

- Build up sales reps' messages.

- Make clients make the following strides (request more data, demand an example, put in a request, etc.); and

- Attract clients to your business.

Your promotion objectives ought to be laid out in your strategy. For instance, you might need to get a specific level of development in deals, create more requests for deals, or work around in-store rush hour gridlock. The ideal outcome can basically be expanding name acknowledgment or altering the picture. Targets fluctuate contingent upon the business and market you're in.

All items and organizations go through three phases, with various publicizing objectives for each.

1. The new company:

You're new on the scene and have to lay out your personality. Your organization needs elevated degrees of advancement and exposure to catch customers' eye.

2. The developing business:

When your character is laid out, you want to separate yourself from your opposition and persuade purchasers that yours is the help or item to attempt.

3. The laid-out business:

The reason right now is to remind customers why they ought to keep purchasing from you.

Regardless of which stage your business is in, promoting follows four stages, as per the business mental helper: "Mindfulness, Interest,

Want, Activity." Your responsibility is to make planned clients mindful that your item or administration exists, provoke their curiosity in how your item or administration can help them, make them need to attempt your item or administration, and lastly, make a move by requesting more data or really purchasing the item.

While fostering a promotion effort, complete the accompanying four-step methodology:

1. Characterize your market:

Figure out who your objective market is (those clients are probably going to purchase your item or service). One magazine that is enjoyable to peruse, fascinating, and supportive in such a manner is American Socioeconomics.

2. Lay out your financial plan:

Understand what you can afford to spend to reach your ideal interest group.

3. Plan which media you'll utilize:

Sort out the most effective ways to reach your imminent clients with your message.

4. Think of a promotion system:

Pick the best message and visuals for your advancing exertion.

SORTS OF ADVERTISING

Understanding accessible advertising channels will assist you with settling on the ideal choices for your business. A fruitful publicizing effort will increase awareness of your business and items, draw in clients, and create deals.

Whether you're empowering new clients to get one of your current items or are sending off another item, your image is bound to stick out assuming that you utilize the right creative (pictures, video, or other promoting designs) in the right climate.

You might find that you obtain the best outcomes by utilizing a blend of channels.

For each publicizing type, consider the following:

- Likely reach
- Cost (media, inventiveness, and creation)
- Source of inspiration (how you believe individuals should answer).
- Papers
- Magazines
- Radio

- TV

- Outside

- Indexes

- On the web

TOP HINTS FOR VIABLE PROMOTING

1. Utilize your particular image 'look and believe' and be predictable.

2. Ensure your inventive idea is enticing and significant.

3. Attempt to engage the faculties and associates on a close-to-home level.

4. Incorporate areas of strength for an activity so clients know what to do.

5. Be dispassionate about channel decisions; center around the client.

6. Coordinate channels so they cooperate and assume their parts.

7. Tailor your inventive execution to suit the promoting medium.

8. Twofold: actually, take a look at the fact that all data is forward-thinking and precise.

9. Guarantee that your publicizing quality mirrors your business quality.

10. Affirm that your publicizing stays in accordance with guidelines.

Begin advertising

There are three vital parts to a powerful promotion effort.

First, Media

Plan, audit, select, and book the space for your chosen channels.

This might include managing delegates from media organizations. Make sure to zero in on your targets and utilize your exchange abilities. For instance, you might get a rebate for booking various spots simultaneously.

Second, Innovative

Figure out the all-encompassing inventive idea for your mission.

In view of your image positioning, remarkable selling point, and client needs, you should concoct the 'large thought' for your promoting effort. This imaginative methodology will incorporate both visual planning and copywriting.

Lastly, Creation

Create and carry out the inventive across all media channels.

You will then, at that point, move onto the crusade,which you will carry out in view of your style rules. Take a higher perspective on the job of various channels and how they cooperate. Also, ensure you supply records on time and in the right organization.

Ensure you deal with your interior correspondences before you go live.

- **Working with outside offices**

Could your business profit from getting proficient assistance to plan and run its public relations campaign?

Be practical about your interior abilities and limits. Consider the benefits and drawbacks of doing it without anyone's help compared with connecting with trained professionals.

- **Measure and investigate**

In the event that you put resources into promoting your business, you really want to know the outcomes.

For instance, suppose you run an infants' shop, and through the arranging system, you set the following for your publicizing effort:

- increment guests to the store by 10%
- support existing item deals by 5%
- keep on further developing brand picture.
- Screen your business.

- Survey the outcomes

- Do a survey

- Publicizing guidelines

Before you start, you really want to comprehend the regulations and guidelines related to promotion.

Your promotion must constantly furnish clients with the 'entire picture'.

- It should be authentic.

- All limits should be authentic.

- The general impression should not be misdirected.

SAVINGS

Setting aside cash in business is significant for various reasons. It can assist you with remaining within your financial plan and letting loose assets to reinvest in the business. It can likewise assist you with developing a stash of assets to use in the event of a surprising cost or income shortage. Setting aside cash guarantees that you have an adequate number of assets to cover costs when times are tight. Setting aside cash assists with guaranteeing that your business stays beneficial and has the essential assets to develop and succeed.

Setting aside cash and planning is an extraordinary method for guaranteeing that your business is burning through cash in a coordinated and effective way. Doing so can assist you with recognizing regions where cash is being squandered, and it can likewise assist you with focusing on which costs are fundamental and which ones can be cut.

Moreover, by planning, you can likewise plan and save for specific business objectives. Using innovation can likewise assist organizations in diminishing costs and setting aside cash. Robotization can assist organizations with smoothing out processes and decreasing costs related to physical work. Moreover, there are various programming programs accessible that can assist organizations with dealing with their funds, like accounting and bookkeeping programs.

CASH SAVING TIPS IN ENTREPRENEURSHIP

1. Exploit free or minimal-cost innovation

This smooths out processes, increases effectiveness, and cuts costs. One model is cloud-based administration, which can assist with mechanizing assignments, diminish regulatory expenses, and save money on extra room.

2. Screen expenses intently

This can be a troublesome yet significant errand to guarantee that your business runs productively and stays within your spending plan. Here are a few hints to assist you with monitoring costs:

- Set up a framework for following costs. This will assist you with monitoring the amount you are spending and where the cash is going.
- Make a spending plan and stick to it. This will assist you in better managing your funds and ensuring

that you are not spending beyond what you can afford.

- Screen income. This will assist you in distinguishing regions where costs can be decreased and in better distributing your assets.

- Track expenses consistently. Regularly practice it by surveying your costs no less than once every month to guarantee that you are on target with your spending plan.

- Put resources into bookkeeping programming or recruit a bookkeeper. This will assist you in effectively following and dealing with your costs.

3. Exploit charge derivations

Duty allowances are a significant piece of business since they can assist with decreasing how much cash organizations need to pay in charges every year. Try to research and exploit derivations for things like business travel, hardware purchases, and different costs. By exploiting derivations, organizations can get a good deal on their duties and become more serious.

4. Reduce out superfluous expenses

Examine your spending plan and costs to recognize regions where you can reduce costs. Lessening costs in business is a significant element in the progress of any association. It is important to guarantee that costs are kept low and under control to increase overall revenues and stay on the lookout.

Cost reduction can be accomplished through various procedures, for example, smoothing out processes, lessening work costs, rethinking specific administrations, and scaling back on superfluous materials and supplies. Furthermore, executing energy-saving practices can likewise prompt tremendous expense reserve funds. Reducing pointless expenses in business can assist associations with staying productive and augmenting their assets.

5. Haggle better terms with providers

Haggling better terms with providers can be a significant part of maintaining a fruitful business. By arranging terms that are better for your business, you can set aside cash to further develop your production network, lessen risk, and make your business more beneficial and economical.

Having a decent comprehension of the market and your providers can assist you with distinguishing regions where you can haggle better terms, for example, limits for mass buys, further developed conveyance terms, or longer installment terms.

Likewise, it is essential to have your very own reasonable comprehension needs and how you can best meet them. By haggling better terms with providers, you can guarantee that you are getting the most ideal arrangement and can boost your assets and benefits.

BENEFITS OF SAVING

Setting aside cash for business can have various advantages. It can provide more prominent monetary security, expanded liquidity, and the capacity to reinvest in the business. Monetary security manages the cost of giving you the inner harmony to zero in on maintaining your business, while expanded liquidity permits you to rapidly make the most of new open doors. Reinvestment in the business can prompt expanded benefits and development, permitting you to extend and enter new business sectors. At last, setting aside cash in business can assist with guaranteeing a more promising time to come for your business, which is what all entrepreneurs are going for.

INVESTING

As an entrepreneur, it pays to be aware of wellbeing nets. Contributing is a judicious method for guaranteeing your business stays secure despite misfortune and shouldn't just help you as an individual; in addition, consider everyone around you, including workers, resources, and clients. Searching out speculations can give genuine serenity that permits business people to zero in on fostering their endeavor with certainty.

You can continuously depend on your assets for later and keep up with the security of those resources. Be that as it may, current bank accounts don't offer sufficient premiums or liquidity to make them an alluring choice any longer. Now is the right time to investigate effective money management choices! Recall that saving actually has its benefits: your well-deserved cash will remain securely concealed on the off chance that you want speedy access down the line.

As an entrepreneur, having a reserve fund and a propensity can provide priceless security with regards to retirement. Not exclusively will this assurance independence from the rat race after your functioning years are finished, yet it likewise gives true serenity while you're developing your business. With these plans set up, business people have something less to stress over, permitting them to center exclusively around the work they're enthusiastic about.

Significance of Investing

1. Individual Monetary Objectives

As the entrepreneur directing your prosperity, it's important to remember that there are a larger number of parts to life than simply work. Contributing a part of what you procure from your business in securities exchanges or shared assets can help support accomplishing individual monetary objectives and guarantee future thriving. Land speculation and beginning another little endeavor may likewise be a choice worth considering for extra revenue gushes not too far off.

2. Crisis purposes

In the midst of an emergency, having a security net can assist with diminishing the weight. A safety effort like an interest in one more resource that isn't connected with your ongoing business can be utilized as an unmistakable advantage when things don't appear to be practical. Rather than being cleared away by conditions, you have the power and opportunity to pick how best to handle monetary or individual issues, whether it's purchasing value, selling speculations, or beginning once more. Contributing is key to overseeing such difficult minutes.

3. Capital for future

Remaining on the ball has never been more significant. With innovation and financial changes occurring at a fast rate, organizations should be ready to develop their methodologies or risk being abandoned. In many cases, speculation is considered to be key to endurance in such questionable times, empowering organizations to fund important updates and redesigns when change can hardly stand by. Regardless of whether no outer elements are driving your business choices, shrewd venture arranging currently could assist with making ready forward later on down the line.

4. Expansion in business

Putting resources into an alternate business, as opposed to keeping all your cash in only one endeavor, is a clever move. Doing so differentiates possible misfortunes and extends open doors for development, prompting more prominent abundance on the scale level as well as actually. Spotting occasional or infrequent benefit-creating areas can give you that additional poke when it comes time to find reasonable organizations and asset them suitably, making fantasies about possessing another organization become reality.

CONCLUSION

What an exciting journey it has been through the pages of "Empire of Innovation: Unleashing the Entrepreneurial Spirit."

Building a business empire through entrepreneurship isn't all about dreaming, reading, and asking questions. All these are important, but without planning and putting to work all you have gotten, the whole process won't yield desirable results.

To build an empire, one needs

1. To dream or have a picture of the kind of empire he or she wants
2. Source for suitable materials
3. Start with a solid foundation
4. And starts the building

You don't start building and go back to sleep. You keep building until you have an exact or better representation of the picture of the empire you have in your mind. So it is in entrepreneurship.

In the chapters of this book, we have been able to dig deep into entrepreneurship. What it means, what it takes to be a unique entrepreneur, what attributes to possess to achieve success in entrepreneurship, the challenges expected, and ways to overcome them.

Now it's time you put to practice all you have learned and become that unique entrepreneur who is causing magnificent changes in the world of entrepreneurship. I strongly believe that if you are willing, dedicated, and focused, you can and will build that great empire you have always dreamed of.

And yes, you can do it!